PAPAL BULLS AND ENGLISH MUFFINS

Papal Bulls And English Muffins:
MEDITATIONS FOR EVERYDAY IN LENT
JOE McCARTHY

Deus Books
PAULIST PRESS New York / Paramus / Toronto

BX
2170
.L4
M32

Copyright © 1974 by
The Missionary Society
of St. Paul the Apostle
in the State of New York

All rights reserved. No part of this book may be reproduced or transmitted in any form or by any means, electronic or mechanical, including photocopying, recording or by any information storage and retrieval system, without permission in writing from the Publisher.

Library of Congress
Catalog Card Number: 73-91372

ISBN: 0-8091-1812-2

Published by Paulist Press
Editorial Office: 1865 Broadway, N.Y., N.Y. 10023
Business Office: 400 Sette Drive, Paramus, N.J. 07652

Printed and bound in the
United States of America

CONTENTS

Foreword 1

Ash Wednesday 3

Thursday after Ash Wednesday 5

Friday after Ash Wednesday 7

Saturday after Ash Wednesday 9

Sunday: 1st Week of Lent 10

Monday: 1st Week of Lent 12

Tuesday: 1st Week of Lent 16

Wednesday: 1st Week of Lent 20

Thursday: 1st Week of Lent 22

Friday: 1st Week of Lent 26

Saturday: 1st Week of Lent 28

Sunday: 2nd Week of Lent 30

Monday: 2nd Week of Lent 31

Tuesday: 2nd Week of Lent 33

Wednesday: 2nd Week of Lent 35

Thursday: 2nd Week of Lent 37

Friday: 2nd Week of Lent 39

Saturday: 2nd Week of Lent 44

Sunday: 3rd Week of Lent 46

Monday: 3rd Week of Lent 48

Tuesday: 3rd Week of Lent 51

Wednesday: 3rd Week of Lent 57

Thursday: 3rd Week of Lent 60

Friday: 3rd Week of Lent 64

Saturday: 3rd Week of Lent 65

Sunday: 4th Week of Lent 68

Monday: 4th Week of Lent 72

Tuesday: 4th Week of Lent 76

Wednesday: 4th Week of Lent 78

Thursday: 4th Week of Lent 81

Friday: 4th Week of Lent 82

Saturday: 4th Week of Lent 84

Sunday: 5th Week of Lent 86

Monday: 5th Week of Lent 88

Tuesday: 5th Week of Lent 92

Wednesday: 5th Week of Lent 93

Thursday: 5th Week of Lent 97

Friday: 5th Week of Lent 99

Saturday: 5th Week of Lent 100

Palm Sunday 102

Monday of Holy Week 104

Tuesday of Holy Week 105

Wednesday of Holy Week 107
Thursday of Holy Week 108
Good Friday 111
Holy Saturday 114

FOREWORD

These pages color our world not light and lively but in 40 shades of gray. The mood of the book is "down" for this is more the tone and temper of our times.

Others may have other ways to dynamite inertia and jog out a slump but I know no other way than page by page to bore my way into the tunnel we are in and announce to the trapped light at the end of the shaft. Like a good dentist I do not fill on decay, but drill through to the nerve of hope.

At this turn of civilization, where roads cross over and ways divide, the world is going through a change of life, to stick our heads in the sand right now is to invite a horrific kick in the pants.

And so the following pages go the route of a bone deep prayer, i.e., "My God, my God, why hast thou forsaken me"!

ASH WEDNESDAY

Save time
Gain time
Kill time
Money is time.
Sunrise! Wake up!
Grab a paper, get to work!
Driving down dreary streets,
Heavy traffic rush . . .
Home again, supper and sleep . . .
Alarm rings!
Hit the floor!
Shower and shave.
Day after day
Life leaks away,
In a whirlpool of coffee breaks.

The loss of being by always doing.
The loss of having by always buying.
The loss of keeping by always getting.
The loss of peace by constant drive.
The loss of home by always moving.
The loss of name by constant change.
The loss of roots by moving wheels.
The loss of love by flying away.
Our house at the end of the run-a-way.
America U. S. A.

Huffing and puffing,
Pushing and shoving;
Hopping off one damn thing,

Bouncing into another;
Barrelling down the highway 60 miles per
   hour . . .
Pull over brother!
Rest awhile.

(2 Cor. 6:2)
"Now is the acceptable time—
Today is the day of Salvation."

THURSDAY AFTER ASH WEDNESDAY

Are you called Christian
After Him whose name was Christ?
Then you are the one they are all talking about,
The one who really loves and cares for others!
Your human relations are charged with so much forgiveness
Your mercy knows no judgment!
You are the one I always hear about,
The one of said disposition,
Who walks a second mile
When only one mile would do.
You, who turn the other cheek
And give generously to those who borrow.
You give your coat as well,
To him who needs your shirt.
You are now on a hunger strike,
You thirst for world justice.
You are the peacemaker,
One of the children of God,
Suffering persecution for the sake of the whole human race.
Oh, I know you well.
I have heard a lot about your kind.
The poor of spirit,
Who have left all
To follow Him.

With what measure do you measure?
For with what measure you measure,
It shall be measured to you
In return!
If the poor of the world asked you for bread,
You would never give them a stone.
If they asked you for fish,
You would never give them a serpent.
You sell what you have and give it to the poor.
Or do you, too, walk away sad and serious,
Like the young man of old?
Because you have too much
Too much you cannot do without.
Shall you too keep life?
Shall you too lose it?
With what measure do you measure?
For with what measure you measure
It shall be measured to you in return!

(Dt. 30:15)
"I set before you life or
death, a blessing or a curse."

(Luke 9:22)
"He who loses his life for
my sake will save it!"

FRIDAY AFTER ASH WEDNESDAY

Lying the other night
On the white sheets
Of a fresh made bed
Watching television
Through my toes
One thought struck me
With the weight of a freight train.
The whole world knows
That the problems of America
Are not bad breath!
B. O.
Or overweight!
Skip the Ads!
Watch the News.
You will see rats in homes,
Poor schools,
Bad housing,
Working mothers,
Supporting deserted children!
In the face of such human wants
Who gives a damn
What way we smell!
Ad-man, tell me please,
Who sponsors the poor?
Who is their press agent?
Who lobbies their cause?
Who is their St. Vincent DePaul?

(Is. 58:6-9)
"This is rather the fasting
that I wish!. . . .
Setting free the oppressed, breaking
every yoke;
Sharing your bread with the hungry
Sheltering the homeless.
And not turning your back on your own.
Then you shall call, and the Lord will answer
You shall cry for help
And He will say:
'Here I am'!"

SATURDAY AFTER ASH WEDNESDAY

In our humble beginnings, the early Christians, for fear of the Emperor met in secret in the graveyards of Rome. (That's 2000 years ago and since then the tables have turned round the other way.) Our master told us if we were meek, we would inherit the earth. By God he was right, we have. The Emperor is dead and the empire is ours. Now we live in the gold coast of the earth along the money belt of the world, handling the controlling shares of the world's trade.

Jesus, our teacher, was never chaplain to the rich. If he took sides at all, it was decidedly with the poor. While we celebrate the fact that He gave us the Key to Fort Knox—I wonder should we stop to worry about the poor, who meet today in secret in the graveyards of the world?

(Is. 58:9)
*"If you bestow your bread on
the hungry—then light shall rise
for you in darkness.
He will renew your strength
And you shall be a watered garden
Like a spring whose water never fails."*

SUNDAY: 1ST WEEK OF LENT

As Americans, these last
   few years
The weight of the world has
   fallen on our backs
We find ourselves in a
   lopsided world
Where we eat too much
And others don't eat
   at all.
Every night the television
   spits our sins at us
The only news is bad
   news
And we feel we are to blame
   for everything.
We are overwhelmed with
   guilt.
Like the man who ran away
From the debts he could
   not pay
We, too, drown our sorrows
   in too much drink.
The young are no better
   than ourselves
In handling our oversized
   world.
They too cop-out in
   drugs
Frankly America's
   problem

At this time may
  not be apathy
But over-responsibility.
What are we to do?
We who have inherited the earth?
To remember, I suppose, that
For six days God
  created the earth
On the seventh day, God rested.
He must have said
As we must sometimes say to ourselves
To heaven with it!
If the Chairman of the Board
  needed rest
What about us?

*"Remember to keep
the Sabbath Day."*

MONDAY: 1ST WEEK OF LENT

America is a pick and shovel country
Our people were exiled here from Europe
The poor who came from the other side
But America was good to them
They went from rags to riches.
It would, indeed, be irony
If we, their children
Became snobs over small differences
A monied people, the kind of rich
The ruling class
Our forefathers ran away from.
Beggars on horseback who forget so soon
The hours our fathers walked
The hard stones, on rainy nights, through dark roads.
Forgetting the hard times come easy with man.
Home safe!
No one tinkers with a system
That ticks in his favor
No one shoots his own santa Claus
On this crest of small success
Will America forget the children of the dust
The poor who haven't made it.
Only they can tell us how goes the American dream
And where does America go from here.
In the new world, man will happen in a new way
If the poor will lead us!

PART II

The world is a bad
   neighborhood to live in!
It got very run down around
   here lately!
Soon the rich will buy
   the moon
Take off from Cape Kennedy
Move away from the rest
   of us
Like they always have
   done before
Take their money and run!
Leaving us their homes
   in Palm Springs
Their offices in
   Wall Street.
It will be nice up
   there
With their own kind
Shooting golf balls
   in the sand
With a hole in one.
No green fees and a token caddy
Taken from the poor
They will ship him home for
   weekends.
As seen from the moon,
The earth will look
   nice at night
Like Harlem with lights.
But the earth is no
   neon sign,

To amuse the few
  who can afford
To get away from it.
The earth is people
And people is what
It's all about!
Rich Man, buy a star
Move out! Go away!
Hole yourself up in
  a Hilton
Away out in space
With dogs and with guns
Preserve your preserves
Keep out of your life
The whole human
  race
Rich man, it is a wet way
  to go.
To wall yourself up
In your own little ghetto
When you lock us all out
You lock yourself in.
And you don't know
What wealth you are missing.
Meanwhile, back on the
  earth
The poor with the poor
The blacks with the black
The young with the
  young
The old with the
  old
Walk hand in hand
  to the door.

Each man holds the
   key
Each one turns the lock.
Down to the short
   strokes
The question is not
How can (I) make it
But will (we)
For we may not!
Actually life is much
   simpler now
It is reduced to
   EITHER/OR
Either we love!
Or we die!

(Matt. 25:31)
"Whatever you do for one of the
least of these brothers of mine,
you do for me."

TUESDAY: 1ST WEEK OF LENT

In the evenings after dark
Sleepy houses tucked away
From rubber burning highways
Light up the darkness through
   the trees
These are the castles of
   the working class.
A dreary street comes alive
Simply because a man is
   coming home.
Here LOVE IS KEY
The spinal cord of the
   human race
The basic vein that
   runs
Through all our lives
By which our nights
   and days
Are tangled up in
   one another.
The lonely ones of God
Find shelter in each
   other's arms.
The weak ones of God
   grow strong with a kiss.
The wealth of our world
   is not in our banks
But in the rich and deep
   warm and wonderful

Relationships we have
   with each other
By which we exchange
   life
And share the universe.
Viva love
That has done away
   with loneliness
And joined our hands
   our hearts
   our souls
   our bodies
With other human
   beings
We were given life
To give our life to
   someone else
To break our bread
With those around our table
Here at home is felt
In this mystery of each other;
A presence larger than ourselves.

PART II

Danny and Judy had butter for their bread.
A comfortable pillow for their heads.
Late nights they drank beer in the den
Watching Johnny Carson
They had it all together
In their own little hideaway
One night they burned incense to the dark:
"Mumbo jumbo, thanks for nothing, God,"
Danny prayed and they both laughed
Then, for old time's sake
Judy lit a candle to St. Jude.
With Tarot cards
They told their fortune.
After that they read poems
For each other
From Rod McKuen.
They believed in nothing any more
They had each other!
But slowly, slowly, through the years
All their irreverences collapsed.
Eerie moments felt alone
The weirdness of so much
That was unaccounted for
The fears it could be lost.
The wonder-full-ness of each other's presence
The Sacrament of intercourse
Seeing together their own child for the first time
It wasn't his, it wasn't hers.
There was something more than both of them.

At the nursery window, in the hospital,
He was crying
And she was crying
They were mystics all the while and didn't know it.
Their child was mystery.
Then Danny's Dad got killed
In his trailer truck.
Their world fell apart
The only word that they could say was God.
The only prayer they could remember,
    was "Our Father."
(Matt. 6:7)

WEDNESDAY: 1ST WEEK OF LENT

These are sullen
  days
Heroes are out of work
America has gone into a
  change of life
Just like that!
We just had it made
Then something awful
  happened
The lights blew
The music died
Yes, we are Americans
But we don't brag
  about it!
Yes, we are religious
  but we have checked out
  our account with the
  holy places.
Yes, we have parents
But they are out of it!
Yes, we are Americans
  running away from home
We have become a nation
  of drifters.
Hitching, lost on lonely
  highways
Our national anthem
Is "give me shelter."
We want to love
We want to give

We want to belong
The question is belong
   to what, and why?
We have lost confidence
In nearly every human cause.
It was in times like
   these
In days of old
That men found need
To build a golden calf.
But then again
It is also true
That in the past
When men got lost
They started out in a
   new direction.
Lost in his journey
   round the world
Columbus found
   America.
What we are going through
   now
Is not,
I hope,
The miscarriage of
   a nation
But the birth of the
   world.

*Like Nineveh of old the
earth today is called
to change her soul . . .*

THURSDAY: 1ST WEEK OF LENT

An old woman's prayer

"O God, don't let me hurt when for weeks on end
I do not hear a word from my children,
Who I know are busy with their children,
As I was busy with them.
When the grandchildren come,
Strike me dumb so I won't miss a
 single word of the wisdom that through
 their new education system
 they know it all so soon.
Help me hold my tongue about the things
I did when I was young.
For God, they don't want to know,
History bores them, and they are the
 first and the only generation on the planet
 earth.
They never ask how much I loved their
 grandfather and the world he wanted for
 them.
The rules of our new society are not written,
But America has made it clear.
Old people, O God, are to be seen not heard.
They are not to speak unless they are spoken
 to.
Oh, the foolish self-importance of
 our self-important selves
But what I would give to be self-important
 again

Young and independent like them
Next social security check I will buy myself
A champagne blond wig
If they won't talk to me at least,
Then they will talk about me!

When you lose the sense of humor and the fight,
They come and carry you away in a basket.
Above all, O God, keep me strong enough
To maintain my independence and not be a
   burden on anyone—for this latter state
   of things would be worse than the present.
When the children call for me to babysit
   YES SIR!
MAY I BE AS FIT AS A FIDDLE."

(Est. 12:14)
*"My Lord, help me who am
alone and have no help
but you."*

PART II

    Inside a dirty window
    Looking down a busy street
    Sits a grandmother saying her prayers
    In a shabby dress sitting on a
        broken armchair.
    The town parade is on today
    And all the town is there
    Gales of music mixed with laughter
    Fill the air.
    But the world forgets that she is there.

    She remembers well parades
    Of bygone days
    Two daughters and a little boy
    (He died in Pearl Harbor)
    With their Mickey Mouse balloons
    Life was full then.
    A busy housewife, her name was Ma!
    Called out loud in awful need
    So many times a day.
    She had a plenty then of what now she lacks
    The want to be wanted
    The need to be needed
    But now it is said, she is too old.

    She is cast aside
    By the rush of the busy crowd
    Alone she wilts on a dying vine
    An unwanted grandmother.

    She drops from her chair and dies
    The parade passes by.

May she rest in peace
The preacher said.
"Rest," thought Margaret to herself,
Under a blanket of flowers,
"The man is mad
I died of rest!
With nothing to do
And no one to do it with!"

FRIDAY: 1ST WEEK OF LENT

Oh Holy Guru tell me please
When does smoking pot turn to shooting speed
Or petty thievery become grand larceny?
Wise man of the east
When do small bribes become big pay-offs
Or social sipping, heavy drinking?
Doctor of medicine, which cigarette will give me cancer
The one before I shave or
The one after I shower?
Every day someone walks away
From where life is at.
When I was young, they used to call it sin
Now it has no name
But it is the same sad ugly thing
Walking out the door
And leaving life behind.
We crutch our weight on dope or money
We hide in highs of sex and booze
We sell our souls for small success
So goes the weekends of our weeks
In a cloud of smoke
Off center and unreal.
Who's to blame!
All we know for sure
Life is strange
She robs those who cheat on her!
Every man needs another stab at life.
Once again to turn back

And touch what's real
And laugh out loud
To find himself among the saved
Amazed by grace, find love at last
Not in the traffic of his own success
Not in the business dinners or the supper clubs
But in the divine presence of those he values most.
God is in that family tonight
Who before going to sleep
As family speak together and say prayers
And in the mystery of each other's lives
Feel deep the mystic presence
Present in their midst.

(Ez. 18:21)
*"Those who turn away
from sin shall live!"*

SATURDAY: 1ST WEEK OF LENT

He who looks your way with favor
    brings out the better you
In a climate of acceptance, you
    blossom like a flower in the sun.
He who believes in you, takes serious what
    you are.
Relaxed in his presence, you come alive
When he looks at you with love.
You can share the excitement you sometimes
    feel
    in being yourself.
He who believes in you, be He God or be he
    man,
    brings out the best in you.
He is your Healer
He is a Savior
Even while you are still a stranger
He has great hopes in you
And because he loves you
In his presence you grow
Like a raisin in the sun.
His love is patient.
His love is kind.
He is always ready to excuse.
He hopes
He trusts,
He endures all things.
His love takes time for you to change
And life happens because he lets
You be the way you are!

Your healer hears your every word.
Reflects back upon what you say.
If he doesn't get your message right,
He asks you to explain.
All you know for certain
Is that when you are talking,
He really loves to listen!
His love brings out what his
Trust believes is there.
Oh blessed is the creative man
He has no "fix it" complex.
He feels no need to judge
By simply listening
He always understands.
Like God he prizes every man,
Like God he honors the freedom of the Will.
Like God his love is given
No strings attached
To be returned in its kind
Or to be crucified.
Blessed is the man who loves
He builds the world!

(Matt. 5:43)
"Oh be perfect as your
heavenly Father is perfect"

SUNDAY: 2ND WEEK OF LENT

As long as human blood flows through
   human veins,
It shall always be recalled how it came
   to pass,
That an outcast people in Egypt once
   believed
That their God was love,
And was sympathetic to their cause.
Stomping straw day in day out in the
   burning sun, making bricks to build
   the useless pyramids,
They thought this holy thought that
   their sad lot was God's concern.
He promised them a promise land far away
   beyond the wilderness.
There was no way out but through the desert.
With naked faith in His blind word these
   people made it.

We are the children of their belief.
They are the forefathers of our faith.

MONDAY: 2ND WEEK OF LENT

In what lost childhood did Judas
   betray the Christ?
And why did he later hang himself?
This question has never been asked.
And consequently this man has never
   been understood.
He was once judged
He has been forever Damned.
He and so, so many more!
Because society finds it easier to condemn
Than to try and understand.
We don't know why some are born to lose
But we do know that others help a lot
To put a man down the road
Of get lost!
While others if they wish
Can move in to help
And stand a man up again
After he has been slugged to the floor

Did Brendan Behan have any friends
   except his drinking ones?
To save him from his drinking fate,
And therefore save himself?
How lonely was Marilyn Monroe
   on her last night?
Could someone have loved her back to life?
Why could no one reach Judy Garland?
Who put her down so bad?
Was there no one who could lift her up?

Listen Humanity!
We can't lose anymore
We have lost too many before!
Because we are better at blasting,
    and damning and hating—
    than we are at listening, loving
    and understanding.

On the graves of those
We never understood
Let us take a stand
JUDGMENT be damned!

(Luke 6:36)
"Be compassionate, as your Father
is compassionate. . . .
Judge not and you shall not
be judged. . . ."

TUESDAY: 2ND WEEK OF LENT

I often heard it said
By my father and my mother
"You can't put an old head
On young shoulders."
Their wisdom was good sense
That no one ever follows.
For parents and teachers
Still insist
On plonking their heads
On their kids' shoulders,
And are still surprised
When they get their heads
 handed back to them.
This system doesn't work
The transplant doesn't take.
All of which indicates
Good education begins not this way
But the other way 'round.
What if we began where the child is
And build from the ground up
Not from the mountains down
But start from the inside out?
Meet the child where the child is,
And as our relationship grows,
Share more of ourselves.
Stand for what he will become
Urging him to reach out for it.

The teacher thus becomes
A listener and by the pupil

He will be taught.
Parents learn fast
There is only one way to stay young
And that is to grow up again
　with their children.
A father grows up with his daughter
And sees through her eyes
The great things he missed
The first time around.
And grandparents growing old
　staying young
Playing with their grandchildren.

This disposition of honest search
　and mutual trust
Will wipe away the awful need
We feel to know it all
And relieve the weight
To prove we are always right
And never wrong.

This is the system
That breaks up all the factions
Where teachers are students
And parents are children
And even preachers hear God
　from their people!

(Matt. 23:1)
"Avoid being called teachers.
The greatest among you
will be the one who serves
the rest."

WEDNESDAY: 2ND WEEK OF LENT

There he is—unlovely and unloved.
Moving from garbage can to garbage can
   sorting junk.
Searching for something,
Anything that would help.

The term, "no good bum,"
   does a terrible injustice to his
   unique experience as a human.
How he feels about life,
And what life means to him!
How he sees a sunset!
A sunrise!
A street light or a cup of coffee.

How high are his highs
On cheap wine on an empty stomach?
How low are his lows,
In hunger and hangover?

Who can stop his inside bleeding?
Undoubtedly he is someone's son,
   even perhaps someone's father.

The crowds pass by,
   they in their world,
He in his.

The question is an open one!
Could someone yet save him?

Love him back to life?
We will never know
For no one ever tries!
We all gave up on him long ago.

We who expect nothing from him
We shall not be disappointed!

(Matt. 20:17)
*"The Son of Man has come
not to be served but to serve."*

Who serves this ripped off
    all time loser?
God's lonely—lonely!
God's lonely—lost!

THURSDAY: 2ND WEEK OF LENT

Do you look away from those who look at you?
How are you present when you are present to others?
Are you open or are you closed?
Have you time for a chat?
Do you stop to make fun?
Do you call on the phone to be there for others, to ask
how they are?
To listen when they talk
and take seriously
what they say?
To suffer their needs,
to sorrow at their wants
and laugh at their jokes?
Have you time for the sidewalk chat?
The serious talk at the coffee shop?
The wave across the street,
The open smile
That tells your friend
You are glad he is here?

> All the little-little things
> That grease the wheels of living
> And keep the show on the road
> Come straight from the human heart!

(Luke 16:19)
"Once there was a . . . man who dressed in purple and lived and feasted splendidly every day. At his gate lay a beggar . . . who longed to eat the scraps that fell from the rich man's table."

FRIDAY: 2ND WEEK OF LENT

We do not know what
   life is
We only know what
   life can do.
We see it in the child
The child who was
   born today.
Small in his cot
Near the wall in his room
There is no word for
   his life
But to live it.
He doesn't understand
He is it.
He will
   Touch it:
   Feel it:
   Chew it:
   Drop it:
   Break it:
   Love it:
And sometimes say Yeah!
I buy it.
Or dammit No!
I can't take it.
Life is understood
   no other way
Except from the
   inside out

By the child who
  is born today!

At first he cried
With awful fear
When first he joined
The human caravan
But cuddled in his
  mother's arms
And fed with a mother's
  milk
He learned fast to
  trust in love.
The love that made him
Make himself
The love that makes
  the world.
(The child who was
  born today.)

Someday soon this
  puny child
Will find his tongue
And say in stuttering
  words
How he feels about
  this outfit.
Soon he will have
  questions of his own.
Questions no one can
  answer
He will sit all alone
In a field open wide

With a frog in his hands
And wonder what makes
   it all happen.
He will whistle and sing
And run through
   the rain.
Others will hurt
   him.
He will cover his
   pain.
He will strike
   back at life
Whose laws aren't
   right.

No one can tell him
The right way to go
He must dig himself
   out
Of the tunnel he is in!
Loving 'til death
The whole damn thing
He will never give up
His own chance to be
The child who was
   born today.
He will not be first
Not surely the last.
Lost in some bar
Late in some town
Who will curse out
   his God.
Who messed up his world.

And next day
On his knees on
   some floor in some room
He will pray!
And doubt all
   his words
And feel so alone
'Cause no one is
   listening
He talks to a wall
The child who was
   born today.
Live life he will
But name he can't.
When all words
   have been said
And there is nothing
   to say
In the book of his tribe
He will read how it was
On this earth
With his people
   before him.
How they wrote
   of the mystery
They felt in their
   life
How they spoke of the
   holy
They felt in their
   blood.
He will read the
   diary

They kept with their
   God
The Bible!
And I believe, he
   will believe
In his own peculiar way,
The child who was born today.

(Matt. 21:33)
*"If only the old could trust
in the young
they would realize
that often the stone which
the builder rejects
becomes the cornerstone."*

SATURDAY: 2ND WEEK OF LENT

There is today a growing bias, mountain size, against the scientific point of view. The young doubt very much that the whole world can be reduced to weights and measures, bought and sold for dollars and cents. They claim that the wholly rational man has lost everything but his mind.

They have left the area of head completely and rely heavily on gut reactions. Because of this, intuitions, feelings and imaginings, poetry and prophecy are back strong for what looks now like a long stay.

All isms are in their syllabus of errors. Quantum theorems, logical abstractions, scientific analysis all have been shafted to the garbage cans.

The occult is revived, astrology is chic, the devils are back from the damned. Witchcraft is doing what it does best, witchery.

Oriental religions are in, with Zen meditations daily on the "UN-MANIFEST."

They wear crosses around their necks, Christ is theirs as he is ours.

The present religious scene has its own kind

of logic and makes its own brand of sense.
Reduced to its irreducible point what does it
all say but that the young, too, believe in
what can't be seen.

They need adults who understand them so
well that the young are loved as they are. The
young will come home to chapel, when they
and our chapels are ready for them.

(Luke 15:1)
*"While he was still a long way off,
the father caught sight of him coming
and was deeply moved. He ran out to
meet him, threw his arms around his
neck and kissed him."*

The Prodigal Son was lucky he had such a big man
for his Daddy!

SUNDAY: 3RD WEEK OF LENT

In the Church today
All bets are hedged,
Heaven is closed
And the clergy are out of work.
The idea of God is still entertained
By half hearted saints
And half hearted sinners.
Religious renewal only lasted
   half a day
Then it fell asleep with
   an almighty snore.
A fog of boredom has blacked out the world
Giving rise to hate so strong
That many would level every church,
And raise up a bowling alley.

The church they shout
Is not a home
It has no word for our experience.

We go there as strangers
We are talked at by strangers
As strangers we leave alienated.

We are a fragmented people
Everyone is on a trip
Doing his own thing;
There is no way to share
With others the excitement
We sometimes feel about being ourselves.

Our human hearts
 that crave belonging,
Must find in the world
A place to belong,
As never before,
We need communion Now!

Maybe it is time
To open up again
The closed question
Of "Someone up there,"
Someone anywhere,
Someone who gives a damn,
Someone to call the family home
Around His holy table.

MONDAY: 3RD WEEK OF LENT

By living life as it was, by calling the shots as he saw them, by being true to what he knew to be true, Jesus Christ set up pins for his own crucifixion! By laying the ax to the root he paid the price of being his own man by his early death.

Patriots felt he was a rebel, the pious said he blasphemed, the holy held he hung around with sinners, the rabbis showed that he was unauthorized, and the gossip had it he was a wino and a glutton.

Yet despite all the rumors and rumblings swirling round his life, common people who had nothing to lose by listening to him, found his wisdom good sense. They loved his parables and put his stories in a book. They wanted to make him King!

He ran away into the hills.

It was not that he was elusive, but a man must do what a man must do in order to be true to what he knows is true!

He who once called Herod a fox and had his share of public spats with vested clergy, knew life was much more complex than his fickle place on their gallup poll.

His stock in trade was honest truth worked out in inner light, the truth that made him free, though he never had it made. Yet he always had that inner consistency by which he called a spade a spade.

Rich cats like Herod and Pilate, who were kept to keep the order and enforce the law, could not appreciate his worth and this comes as no surprise to us that those of vested interests are often blind and out of touch with the really real!

But that holy men, paid to be good, were so deeply implicated in the complicity of his crucifixion; this anomaly leaves us forever wondering about ourselves!

This we know that the truth is still made flesh and lives amongst us in the strangest human packages. The question is how do we handle it? Kill it? Or live it?

Up to now our record shows that our strongest suit has been mass conformity and blind compliance with social demands. Our hands have been short in the trumps of loyal dissent and conscientious objection.

At this turn of civilization, when eye-serving service has brought us so close to a near miss, we are forced into a soul-searching quest.

By dint of present circumstances, chances are

we shall now become truer disciples of the inner consistency so reminiscent of our Lord and Savior, Jesus Christ!

TUESDAY: 3RD WEEK OF LENT

In an age that agrees on very little, most people concur that what we need most of all is leaders! Yet the record shows how short in luck our past has been in this regard.

God knows we have had our share of self-anointed autocrats who took our planet earth into their hands and promised us a promised land.

Little Caesars obsessed with messianic causes have taken our world by storm and drowned our world in baths of public blood. They were the Hitler kind, tantrum children, of infant minds, who acted out their inner needs upon the stage of history.

They were goaded on by the roaring crowds and by popular demand. They had, or so they felt, a mandate from people. Devils, they were, who prayed in chapels and were accountable to no one, not even to God. They have set up many crosses and filled many graves across the world but they have not been capable of raising one notch of the quality of our human condition.

Oh men, beware of the God-sent man who has come to put us all together. Beware the savage messiah. We are not his concern, he is his own issue; he is a driven man; his path is glorybound; our vote is only a feather for his nest.

Mark him well; he cannot take an honest no! And is never sure of what he is certain. He has ways and means of wiping out all opposition. He assigns to beds of clay those who cannot buy his packaged plan for guaranteed success. The future is a one way street and he has total charge of all the traffic. Such a man should not be a leader of other men. He would be good for quarrying stones! There he could be objective—in total control of rocks.

> In an upside down world
> Stuck together backwards;
> Where God creates idiots,
> The only way one can live or love
> Is to accept the fact that the whole system
> Is only half formed!
> All is still in the fetus stage of its own becoming

On the rugged cross
  of love
Each human pain delivers
The newly born.
Watching the hour hand of the clock
Fulfillment comes to those who work and wait

All that is becoming, still becomes.
Amazing grace creates through time in space
Dynamic is the growth of every growing man.

In the ages of eternity it is but yet the dawn

Side by side by God—man is but
   in the childhood of his years.

So far, so good, it all works
It delivered us!
Do we accept as certain and truly feel
The creative role we are called to play in a
   world
   half born
   half made
   half there
   half finished
   half fulfilled.

In such a world put together backwards
Let the restless leader
   rest tonight
Taste life
And say to his soul—
   peace.
Laugh at himself
Relax with a beer
Sing a song with the crowd
The crowd who hope!
The world will be a better place
If we know how to celebrate
While God waits!

PART II

If Plato was King of the world and Socrates President of America, if Pope John was Pope again, and Dag Hammarskjold head of the United Nations then this planet would be in the hands of the brightest and the best—who would doubt their acknowledged wisdom? And what of those who would buck their plans to usher in Utopia? If these Giants ruled the world would they be big enough to honor dissent? Would they who were ahead of their time tarry with those who fell behind? Would their visions of genius wait patiently on each one's uniqueness and take seriously human differences? Or would they of so much light ride rough shod over those whose only light is darkness, and leave behind all nay sayers bleeding, dying? Standing here in human history where roads divide, forcing the future as a few see it, is not the human way to go.

Whether Pope or President, Parent or Priest
The leader meets the people
where the people are,
After that they will follow him anywhere
They might even crucify him.
He digs them.
They dig him.
He lights their fires.
He scratches where they itch.
He speaks to their situation.
He verbalizes their feelings.

He is steeped to the teeth in their experience.
His power over them
Is their fear of missing a word.
He is on their wave length.
Not only does he know them
He knows well the world they left outside
The tone and temper of their times
The prevailing bias of their culture
The spirit of their age
How they experience their existence
What is their self-understanding of
 themselves.
His words are his life
And are as real as his touch with his people.
When he speaks they are saying to
 themselves
"Dead on brother"! "I love this guy!"
"He really knows me."
He meets them where they are
Gives them what they will take.
As his relationship grows
He shares with them more of himself
He stands for what they can become
He urges them to reach out for it!
He watches for feed back
That says he is "out of it."
He is a listening learner
A teacher by his pupils taught
His antennas are always out
What is heard is well-received
Before returned.
Everything he says is a response
To everything that he hears them say
Filtered through his own experience.

Fascinated listener
He plays back to them
His own thoughts on what they think.
He works always from the inside out.
Never from the mountain down.
Forever and always
The leaders boast
Is as it was
   "in illo tempore"
"I know mine and
   mine know me"
The leader knows
   his people
He delivers door to door
And often with his life
Pays the price
Of coming too close to
   home.
Possessed by a
   prophet's vision
The test of any leader
Is his ability to love
   to "70 X 7" . . . .

(Matt. 18:21)
"Forgive his brother
from his heart."

WEDNESDAY: 3RD WEEK OF LENT

Perhaps the hardest cross of all to bear these days
  Is the wall between the pulpit and the pew.
The young, they stay away in droves,
  Is the Church to blame?
What is it they want we do not have?
  We sense our own irrelevance and smell our own decay.
Ready-made creeds and hand-me-down codes,
Force-fed to the young, cannot be done.
  The same repeated answers will not interrupt
  the protest of their living question.
Give us, they say, our own stuttering attempts to pray.
From our own experience let us state clearly who
  and why we are.
Stammering, let ourselves define the divine.
For God, they say indeed accommodates Himself to His growing child.
Ours and ours alone must be the words by which
We call Him Father, for despite all that is fair or foul about our times,
Yes, by God, we are the Sons of God.

Yes, there is a different kind of cat (these days)

Standing at the back of Church.
And it takes a new kind of sermon to make him purr.
We do not grudge them Lord their own demands
But did it have to happen when we were tops
In the old school of thought?
We do not question their questions.
But the answers we answer with, they do not want.
When, then, we question them,
They have no answers either.
They say we talk in jargon that speaks naught about
Their loves, their laughs, their secret schemes,
Their ideals and mad young dreams.
Surely be to God, Jesus Christ, Himself
Is not divorced from what they value most.
No they made him a Superstar and a Godspell.
And they tell us, his messenger,
We have lost the message.

O God, give us the wits to sctatch where these people itch
Talking God to one another
will never be the same
Since the gang from Sesame Street came.
Yet, what they ask is a very simple thing
That what we pray and what I say in Church makes sense.

Surely that is not asking too much
Hopes are high they will teach us yet
To say again the word of God in the words of
~~men.~~ humans

(Dt. 4:1—Matt. 5:17)
*"Do not forget the things
which your eyes have seen
. . . but teach them to
your children and to your
children's children."*

THURSDAY: 3RD WEEK OF LENT

I do not know, so help me God
If wars be right or war be wrong!
But once I stood beside a widow,
At the burial of her man
She held his last letter in her hand
And read it out for those around!
"Yesterday I flew five hundred feet above a village
Releasing bombs on chimneys, roofs and every moving thing.
I saw the smoke, I saw the dust, the rising flames
But heard no human cry,
Felt no human loss,
Saw no drop of human blood
I flew back to the base and left them dying.
The village looked unreal, like an architect's model,
Killing doesn't seem like killing anymore
It is just a game,
Like shooting sitting ducks in a shooting range.
Technology has made war cold and clean
But it is still the same sad ugly thing
Unworthy of the human heart.
If I could look into their eyes
Before I did it. I would never do it.
Because I die each time I realize
These people love each other like "I love you."

Ah! Speed the day
I will be home.
Then I can be human
In another way.
A husband first
And a father mighty soon.
I love you, love;
Wait up nights for me.
Now it won't be long.

PART II

No more war never no more!
Ask not for whom the siren blows
It blows for man
He took his life by his own hand
They said it would never happen
But it did. Each body lies where it fell
The dead can't bury the dead
He who lived by the sword
Died by the sword.
A watergate man in charge of atom bombs
Pushed the button and brought the curtain down.
No one won, everyone lost
The world is a grave
Lifeless, like the moon
The sun is up, but man is asleep.
Day or night the world
Is a barren street
The rest is silence.
There is no pulse
The heart has stopped
The earth is deaf and all its laughter mute.
Her songs are sung and all her children sleep.
Power was the name of the game
Peace was always the cause
The dream of peace is real
But the dreamer is dead!
No more war, never no more!

(Luke 11:14)
"When a strong man fully armed guards his country, his possessions go undisturbed . . . but when someone stronger comes he carries off the arms on which he relied. . . ."

FRIDAY: 3RD WEEK OF LENT

When Christianity happens
   it is such a stranger
We call it by a special name,
We call it a saint.
Dumbstruck by the phenomenon
   of Francis of Assisi
Our only reaction is
"My God, it works."
The rule of sainthood will
   never change.

(Mark 12:28)
"You shalt love the Lord
your God
With all your heart,
With all your soul,
With all your mind,
With all your strength,
And you shall love your neighbor
   as yourself."

All the fuss and feathers
   of the world East and West
Are here reduced to two questions
How deep is our touch with Him,
How deeply are we in touch
   with others?

SATURDAY: 3RD WEEK OF LENT

A very religious man went into his
 church to pray and he prayed thus:

"Thank God I am not like the rest of men!
I have all the personality, they are so dull
I am a great singer, they can't carry a tune
I am so bright, they are so dumb
I have all the contacts, they don't know a soul
I know all about it, they don't have a clue
I am so rich, they are so poor,
I am so cultured, they are bores
I am in—they are out,
I am a swinger, they are squares.
Thank God, I am not like the rest of men
I am white, they are black."

PART II

Looking back over our shoulder
Back 350 years
Back to where America began
The land was covered from coast
  to coast
With mighty trees.
The problem was the harvest was
  too great
And laborers too few.
The black man of Africa
  was the answer.
1619, before the Mayflower
They were brought here
To harvest tobacco in Virginia
Cotton in Carolina
Sugar in Louisiana
They chopped down the tall
  pines of Georgia
They tilled the hard soil
  of Mississippi
And planted the orange
  groves in Florida.
From sun up to sun down
They worked
And cultivated wilderness
Through their work
  well done
And their free labor.
They, more than any other
  race
That ever came here,
Have made America

What she is today
   a world power.
They fought in every war.
They loved this country well
Their patriotism
Comes up to surprise
In every page of history
Yet America has been to them
A mother of strange disposition
She always favored her
   white child
And has always looked down
   her nose at her black one.
This is a story
Sad and great
Of the black man full of hopes
Who has kept his faith
In a promise never kept.
And still keeps hope.
His cotton-picking hands
Were never paid.
But his love still waits
Before the torch is past. . . .

(Luke 18:9)
"I give you thanks, O God,
that I am not
like the rest of men."

SUNDAY: 4TH WEEK OF LENT

It is little wonder
That with great love
We humans made it up
   from mud.
It is little wonder
That God's delight is
   to be with the children of men.
As those who know us well
Know that we are
   a most delightful outfit.
You see us on the subway
You meet us on the street
You live with us in your homes.
We, the *battered broken beautiful*
   ones of God
Battered, because we have been
   walked on by others.
Broken, because we have let ourselves
   fall.
Beautiful, because in the gutter
We reach out for the stars
Slugged to the floor
Knocked to the ground,
Round after round, bout after bout,
We rise every day return to the ring
Only to be knocked down again.
And come back for more.
How could anyone hate such gluttons
   for life
Such a lust to live!

We never had a golden age
There never will be one
Human life in its better times
Was always a mixed bag
   of mixed blessings

When Columbus saw
The sun go down
On the last landmarks of Europe
He must have died a thousand
   times with doubt.

But a new world
Paid back in full his blind hopes
And made up, indeed, for all his fears.
In these minutes of our experience
In these mountains of our doubt
Can America now afford
To fall apart into 200 million
Broken pieces of human plasm?
No one can stop us now
But we can stop ourselves
America, you never had
   a problem
You couldn't solve!
America, when the people
   turned your wheels
There never was a wall
   to stop you!
We have no reason
   now to doubt
Your ability to find your
   way out
Of the tunnel you are in.

We were never here
   before
There is no map to
   where we are going!
These are our funky
   years.
But these, too, are the
   good old days.
It all depends on
   our ability
To ask the right
   questions
And take the biggest step
We ever took.
Criticize ourselves
Wonder out loud
   with one another
Is this the way to go?
Or are we down the wrong
   road?
The only mistake we made
   in the past
Is that we could make
   no mistake.
We who were so good to
   everyone
Could do no wrong!

Now we know for sure
We are not always right.
What is more, we don't
   have to be!
Sometimes to self-doubt
   and say no

Take its own kind of
  courage.
Dissent is another brand
  of love
The vital test of any
  human outfit
Lies in its members' freedom
  to disagree.

America, go back to
  your roots
You have grown too big
  for your boots
Your future lies not
  with any infallible elite
But as it always has from
  the beginning
With the man on the street.

MONDAY: 4TH WEEK OF LENT

Old man I love you
But how can I tell you
Your world is yesterday
Mine is today
We sit together
   often
In restless silence
Staring into television
Drinking beer
And watching football
On a Sunday
Like it used to be Pa
When you and I were
   young!
Pa, I love your
   calloused hands
They paid across the
   board
For my college education
Yet it is the same
   degree in arts
That makes me a
   stranger in your house.
One dream drove you
   constantly
To cushion hard reality
   for your children
And make the world
   kinder to our lot
But, Pa! your grandson

Will soon forget
Who gave him
What he has got.
You are not surprised
By the world's loss
  of memory
Your love was blind
  with hope
For in your heart
  you know
Your grandson
Has his grandpa's good.
He, too, has dreams
He, too, will give
That others too may get.
For the spirit of the old
Is born in their young.
The apples fall not
  far away
From the family tree!
Pa, I love you still
Once my God Almighty man
Now my falling tree
A lot has changed
And change has
  changed us all
This commandment stays

HONOR THY FATHER!

PART II

What we think of the old
Is how we feel about ourselves
Unless our minds destroy our minds
We must all soon in a very certain way
Come to grips with the phobia of age
That our times have associated with
growing old.
If the acceptance of ourselves depends
Upon bosom measurements and our muscle
tone
Then in other words to be at all we must
be sexually prime.
And after 30 we are over the hill and down
the other side.
All society is screaming at you every day
You are less a woman, less a man.
Don't tell anyone your age.
Look young! Look Young!
You are slipping! You are going! You are
gone!
If you and I are going to live at all,
with any kind of peace
We must believe in all that is happening to
us now, what life is doing to us, follow
where it leads us.
There will be no joy in the soul of America
until we value the grace of age.
For no matter what age we are, we still can do
what matters most.
We can be present to others, and light up
their lives with our offered love.

There are still some crowded hours of
 glorious life before our eternal rest.
If only we give up the struggle to be young
 and let go and live.

(Is. 65:17)
*"For lo, I am about to create
new heavens and a new earth;
he dies a mere youth who
reaches but a hundred years.
They shall live in the houses
they build and eat of the
vineyards they plant."*

TUESDAY: 4TH WEEK OF LENT

You can put a man down,
  look down upon a man,
Keep a man down,
But somehow or other he
  manages to rise
  in furious form.
What I feel is this:
  that the human race is like
  the unsinkable Molly Brown.
Deep bedded in our bones is
  the divine drive
  of magic invincibility.
We have come from the caves,
We have landed on the moon.
Irrepressible was our journey
  to freedom.
Violent was our history,
  no one ever stunted our
  growth who later did not
  pay the price in great sorrow
  of animal wars.

Law and order men were always
  shocked by violence,
  but never asked themselves
  if justice denied over the
  longer haul of history is not
  the cause of great anger,
  that bursts out all over
  when all hell breaks lose.

Reason then is not the spoken
   language.
Hold your tongue in silence
   and work quietly for peace.
Peace is a place in the human heart.
And there never ever will be
   peace while other men
Keep other men in their place,
   and block their progress,
   by stunting their growth.
Whether this happens in a family
   with a child,
   or in the world with a people
   the storms of frustration gather,
   the tides of aggression rise,
   and the floods of evolution come
   to wash away and destroy
   all the once and would be Pharaohs!

(Ez. 47:1)
*"Wherever the river flows,
every sort of living creature
that can multiply shall live and
there shall be abundant fish . . .
Along both banks of the river
fruit trees of every kind will
grow . . .
Every month they shall bear
fresh fruit . . .
For they shall be watered by
the flow from the sanctuary. . . ."*

WEDNESDAY: 4TH WEEK OF LENT

Another sunrise, another day we rise to wash and kiss involvement with our world; deeply dedicated to what we do, we believe the mystery we are in though we shall never ever understand!

There are those, of course, and bless them for it who see no mystery in our being nor puzzle why we are. They are not obsessed by the wherefore of our life, they seek no meaning in the journey of the Universe. Content to live with questions, they quietly settle for the menu of the world.

Life begins and ends for them with a cigarette, a cold beer, a pay check, a good week-end now and then, and of course, the kids. Going home and going to bed.

But others like ourselves stay up nights figuring out the inside story to the face of things bugged by what is really real and what it's all about.

We cannot take the world for granted. It must be questioned for its answers. Even if its only answers are irreducible mysteries.

Life is hard on us, we suffer in our comings and goings and yet despite it all we love this chance to be! Unless our minds deceive our minds the search is ever on for another side to life than what we see.

We are nomads who never settle, a restless stirring moves our souls, some call it grace, but in the main it is the widespread hope that our cruel world has a heart. A heart that prizes people not in numbers only but by name, like Martha, Mary, Abraham.

No one lives who saw His face, yet He echoes a fundamental call in all.

Some say lo! He is over there, others fight saying no! He is over here! What matters most I suppose is that each man hears him call his name out loud in the silent mountains of his mind. The haunting call that will not go away.

Religion is never God slapping us across the face waking us up to his presence.

> Religion is a belief simple as it is sound
> That existence will not betray us
> That the good things of life are real
> That love is true and life will last
> That our desires will not be deceived
> That our instincts of God are well taken,
>   and should be seriously received
> In the same way
> As our eyes see
> And our ears hear

We ought to buy what our insides feel
We ought to believe.

This means that life has its own kind of logic, makes its own brand of sense; though often unfair, its laws aren't right, yet deep in our veins there is a rhythm we can trust.

There is a presence here full of a reality so great that our minds cannot hold it, larger by infinity than our ability to speak of it, longer by eternity than we can now talk about it.

In this crowded hour each human carries in his heart his own peculiar trust. We may be no mystics, but each one believes the mystery we are in. That's Religion.

(John 5:17)
"My Father is at work
until now."

(Is. 49:15)
"Can a mother forget
her infant?
Even should she forget
I will never forget you!"

THURSDAY: 4TH WEEK OF LENT

Wise men of the East and of the West always said
that God was everything we were not.
When he appeared he was everything that we are.
Born a baby in a stable he died wiped out upon a cross.
He was everything we always wanted to know about God
but we were afraid to ask!

(John 5:31)
"It is not" he said "that
I accept human praise.
It is simply that I know you
and you do not have the love
of God in your hearts
I have come in my Father's name
and you do not accept me."

FRIDAY: 4TH WEEK OF LENT

1. Who was Jesus and why did they say such awful things about him?
2. If Jesus stood for good, how come he provoked in men such evil?
3. If Jesus stood for love, why did he generate such hate?
4. If Jesus is what life is all about, how come humanity did not welcome him with open arms?
5. Why was his message so removed from life that those so close to God sought to have him crucified?
6. What were the real charges against the real Jesus? What were the issues?

1. He prayed that the world would be one.
2. He asked strangers to be friends and he asked us all to love our enemies.
3. He asked those who had to give to those who had not.
4. He asked those who were hit on the face to turn the other cheek.
5. He asked those who harbored hate to leave their gifts at the altar and go first and make peace with their brother.
6. He asked us to love our neighbors as ourselves!

(John 7:1)
"At this, Jesus, who was
teaching in the temple area,
cried out:
'So you know me,
and you know my origins?
The truth is I have not come of myself.
I was sent by One
and Him you do not know.
But I know Him
because it is from
Him I have come'."

1. He is the way into how things are!
2. He is the love behind it all!
3. His is the life where life is at! In Him our hands have touched the base of things. Our eyes have seen the light. The world's secret is here made known.
4. This is the moment He comes through to us!
5. Now we know what God is up to in our world. He touches us and we touch Him, in the powerless love of a helpless servant.
6. He washed with love the feet of others and asked of his followers the same kind of loving service.
7. This is the way, the truth, the life!

SATURDAY: 4TH WEEK OF LENT

Drink to men who came before time
Socrates, Jesus, Gandhi, Martin Luther King
It was a case not so much that the
world was wrong
It is just that they were right
By the times and by the tides
They were asked by God
To talk of things that others
    could not see
To draw a map to where
We had never been before.
From their mother's womb
They were called,
To guide the world out of the
    tunnel we were in.

God's gift to man today
Is the man ahead of our times
His light must never be
An axe to grind with those who
    cannot see.
He must not stoop to cry in beer
That stunted men misunderstand him.
Though Prophets are a God
Man will always kill them.

Drink to the prophet of our day
Who takes his stand
And calls the play
With graveyard face

His honest eye must wink
To all who mourn doom
In the cracks of human hands
He reads the fortunes of tomorrow
He sees too much into things
To fret over guise and argue
 over shadows.
His soul has married life
And even if the sky should fall
His bone deep trust in love
Will always have the final word!
The question for us then
Is a mighty one:
A question asked before!

(John 7:40)
*"Would the Christ be
from Galilee?"*

For we are still the sons of those who
killed the prophets
The sons of those who killed
the Son of God
Who is our prophet now?
Who shall lead us?

SUNDAY: 5TH WEEK OF LENT

Rusty crosses fallen down
On nameless graves,
Grown wild with age,
Tell how men,
In ancient times,
Met cursed fate,
With human hopes.

Their tears were no less bitter
than our own.

Their fears were just as great.

Life was not easy then,
It is not easy now.

Lying dying,
Upon their dying beds,
Parting with their clan,
In flickering candlelight,
They whispered to the dark
Abba—Abba
Allah—Allah
Father—Father
My God—My God
DO NOT FORSAKE ME!

As long as man can believe in death
And celebrate at funerals
I will be there.

Holding on to each other terrified at
the graveyard
We salvage with love
What chaos has destroyed
Giving the family left behind
The heart to trust again
That life and love goes on!
Friends gathered around a grave
Is the hope held out
Above the dead
That the love that lays them down
In a bed of flowers
Is rivaled by a greater love
Waiting for them on the other side!

MONDAY: 5TH WEEK OF LENT

In the stillness of a silent night, a baby cried, a child was born, his name was Jesus Christ. Unless our holy Scriptures lie, he entered human history through a stable door. It was not exactly a break-in as much as it was an inside job. By that I mean what God was up to in our world up to then God was up to in Jesus Christ; that is reconciling the world to Himself.

Even now, two thousand years after the incarnation, man still suffers from that same inferiority complex about our human condition. Secretly, we all feel that our lives are too grubby and puny; too shabby and shoddy for such a divine presence as Jesus Christ. Yet it is the pleasure and pride of man forever that God sits at our table, eats our bread, drinks of our wine, and that he lived our life, died our death without even a halo around His head, to set Him apart from us, the common crowd. He was a working man's man, a simple person among simple people. To prove to the world that man is His central interest, He becomes Himself a man. Whoever would conceive of God as a carpenter by trade, making cradles for expected babies, and finishing wooden plows for farmers waiting to till their fields?

The eyes of man had been strained from searching the skies for the face of God; his ears had long given up the hope of hearing His voice. Then suddenly too surprised to appreciate what was happening to us, we heard from the lips of familiar flesh, strange words of authority and divinity, assuring words of certainty and truth.

(John 8:12)
"I am the light of the world. He who follows Me does not walk in the darkness, but will have the light of life."

The faces that looked up at His and listened to His words that day, were bronzed by the sun and hardened by the ocean spray; yet they beamed with that warmth of love that comes from honest toil. They were farmers and fishermen; by day they dug their fields, by night they fished the deep. Like all men of all times, they cut their bread and spread their butter by the sweat of their brow. Their daily struggle was for bed and bite, just to eat and just to sleep.

From east to west from north to south the news is out that God has set aside the trappings of Divinity and has become a suckling of humanity. In crowded subways, on busy streets, between lonely prison walls everyone knows how God has stooped to conquer man. He no longer lives above our heads in His own misty heaven outside the world, beyond the milky way. No, God was made flesh and dwelt amongst us. Surely, no event of history is fraught with such dramatic appeal, and so freighted with consequences for all mankind.

Willy nilly, Christ has generated in the world a mood of familiarity between God and man and showed in His person the ways of God with human beings.

We feel more comfortable with the world, it is our home now that we know God has a heart.

O God, we need to be your family now. We are all so fragmented! So broken! So lonely! So lost!

A faithless world needs faith; a hopeless world needs hope, a loveless world needs love; it was precisely to bring us faith, hope and love, that He is here. Jesus gives life a plot, a pattern, a purpose, a goal, a reason, a cause, a mission, a destiny, and we the meaning seekers, the question askers look at His conclusions and settle for His answers.

Human history according to His life and death is not an endless series of aimless tragedies, not a totally disconnected train of man's successes and disasters, for through its chapters runs a main thread of purpose, a long term plan, that is a continual fulfillment of God's creative will. Somehow or other it all works out in the end; it all adds up; the puzzle fits. In the contradiction of a cross.

TUESDAY: 5TH WEEK OF LENT

The Son of God became the Son of Man, so that as a human on this earth He could do the good that we overlook or take for granted. If we learn anything from His coming we learn at least the frightening potential and the fantastic possibilities of human presence.

Because of Him our views of man are greater and our sympathies are deeper.

The Bible and the daily news are not reports of different and separated worlds, their subject matter is man, and Jesus Christ has cast his lot with everyone and is identified with every human story.

(John 8:21)
"You belong to what is below,
I belong to what is above.
You belong to this world,
a world which cannot hold me . . .
The One who sent me is with me.
He has not deserted me
since I do always what pleases him."

WEDNESDAY: 5TH WEEK OF LENT

> In Christ, God's love had a human heart;
> God's pity a human face;
> God's power a human form;
> God's presence in the world was in the presence of Christ
> Face to face with Him we are eye to eye with God.

In Christ we discover what God is like, through Him we know what man should be. He enables us to see ourselves as God sees us, that is to see ourselves as we truly are in total reality.

Human response is never aroused by an impersonal God, distant in time, remote in space, but by one who gives himself to us in our human flesh.

Christianity was born and raised in the human situation where the word was made flesh and dwelt amongst us.

The Bible is all about people. All human life is there between its covers. Pride and prejudice, war and segregation are told, not in abstract statements but naming names and citing places. Religion is always in the human situation. In Bethany—in Calvary—with Peter, Paul or Judas. The final answer to the human mystery lies in this. That God lives in those who love.

God flung Himself, through Jesus Christ, into the mainstream of human struggle and allowed it to work its worst upon Him.
He was a victim of the unpredictable laws of nature and the foul use of man's freedom. He was wide open to all the slings and arrows of outrageous fortune. He knew the bitter struggle for bed and bite, the blunt reality of death's destruction, man's bald aloneness even in a crowd. Incredible as it is, we find Him in this whirlpool of human activity, bound to the heaving waters of human destiny, the interflow of tears and laughter, the saga of trial and error, caught in the cross fire of faith and doubt in the joys and sorrow of search but never find.

Well might He know us as a race of distracted humans, forgetful of essentials, neglectful of necessities, drop outs from reality, earth-bound, time-bound creatures numbed by the drab duty of daily drill. Yet since He Himself was here, we can no longer claim that He doesn't know or doesn't care what happens to mankind. Emmanuel! Say what the name means. God with us. Without Him, we would feel locked out of life, without that vital key that makes sense of all this nonsense. With humble pride we realize that man is much more than a crawling insect lost in mountainous debris or the accidental child of an accidental world; instead we are the special sons of a loving Father, who, with watchful eye and a Creator's pride, smiles amusedly at our attempts to love, which we do like a child learning to walk, falling back many times upon our own selfishness.

Because of Him, there is reason for our trying, there is sparkle in our life, hope in our step, confidence in our future, sense in our sorrow, purpose in our pain. Human life upon this planet will never be the same as it was before He came. Now, we are convinced that God shares our laughter and our tears, He joins with us in all our songs and in all our sorrows. He shares with us our life, our death, our heaven, because He Himself like every man became a tragic figure in a world where tragedy is common-place. He was the ideal man in our world, demonstrating to us what He thought a man should be, cut like Himself from the hardest stone in this human enterprise. He did not ask us to do anything He Himself would not have done, and so He carried His cross like every other man, showing by His life what He demands of us. In Him were embodied the many splendored mysteries of life and love, of human drama and bitter struggle. He knew the blistered weariness of tired feet and the sweaty hunger of a thirsty carpenter. A God He was but a man as well who was beaten, lynched and crucified.

His life has the weight and ring of true metal. The Gospel story is so true to life that anyone could read the same incident in tomorrow's daily news. No myth or legend would be written so of any God. Born a baby in a stable, crucified a criminal on a cross. Such a God is a contradiction in terms, but is not all life one great paradox? He spoke of love and lived it. He begged for love and gave it. He sanctified suffering and used it to save the world. He died as He had lived "doing good," practicing what He preached, forgiving those who crucified Him.

Without Him, man is cut off from God and left alone with man in gathering terror, in choking fear.

Without His real presence, our only sacrament is suicide.

Jesus said it all when he said it thus:

(John 8:31)
"Were God your Father
you would love me
for I came forth from God
and am here. . . .
It was He who sent me."

THURSDAY: 5TH WEEK OF LENT

The wordless wonder in a baby's eyes
The awful fear in a dead man's stare
It is no wonder I wonder
What it is all about.

The world is old and I am new.
The world is big and I am small.
I am only one among three billion more,
But I am I, and this, you see, makes all
   the difference to me.
Cabined in my cell, imprisoned in my shell
Life can be for me a happy heaven or a
   lonely hell.
No one ever wore my skin, so no one will
   ever know,
What fun I had, what tears I shed,
What thoughts tiptoe around my head.
What things I feel but dare not say,
What sorrows eat my heart away.
Perhaps, they think I smile, when I dwell
   within my soul,
An isolated island in an undiscovered sea.
When I step off the world, will it stop?
How am I to know that it goes on without me?
In this sense I am all there is, for after
I go there is nothing!
Oh yes, there will be spring and other
   summer days,
But I shall not be here!

Ah! there's fear when I am dead,
Shall I still be me?

While I was here,
I tried to speak,
But words would not convey
All that I was and that I saw,
All that I felt and all I had to say!
Being unto myself,
Afraid of what I am,
Is this a feeling felt
By everyman?

And then Jesus said:

(John 8:51)
*"I solemnly assure you
if a man is true to my word
he shall never see death.
Before Abraham came to be
I am."*

FRIDAY: 5TH WEEK OF LENT

Yesterday was one of those days
One of the kids kept me up all night
The night before
I over-slept
I blew a tire
I missed the train
I was late for work
I meet the boss going
Out the door as I was coming in.
My phone was dead
The Xerox went on fire
I forgot my lunch
I had no money to go out!
To cap it off
There was a memo
Sent from management
To say
They were phasing out my department
It was the kind of day
You knew for sure
Christ died for you!

(John 10:31)
"I am God's Son."

SATURDAY: 5TH WEEK OF LENT

In the North Side of Chicago
Going back a hundred years
You enter the spirit of another time.
All the people there
Were emigrants from eastern Europe.
They spoke in broken English
And talked to God in Latin.
Seeing their mighty churches now
Rise against the sky
Scarcely a block apart
You begin to understand
How these humans felt
Away back then
About what mattered most
About themselves.
The magic in their mystery
The holy in their blood.
These puny people said in mighty churches
What touched them deep inside.
These chapels were the fall-out shelters,
Where they ran from chaos
And often cried for total loss,
Or bargained all day with statues of St. Jude.
Don't mock their simple piety
For sacred is the fragile meaning found
By any human in his frail existence.
Worry not about what might have been!
In the quality and texture of their lives
If only they knew then what we know now!
Christ was theirs as He is ours.

Whether He made more sense to them
Than He does to us
Matters very little now.
Only hopefully that
We on our departure
From the world
Will have sacrificed as much
If not more!
To make this land more human
And man more kind.
One question, however, is posed by their life style.
Since the building of churches is no longer chic
What monument rises to our mission
How do we dramatize
Who? Why? and
What we are!

(Ez. 37:21)
*"My dwelling shall be with them:
I will be their God and they shall
be my people . . .
when my sanctuary shall be set up
among them forever."*

PALM SUNDAY

O Clock of life
You two-faced liar
You promised me so much
You did not deliver
You kept me at night
Waiting for my day
Life was just another lap away
Just around the corner.
Waiting for some future glory
I have been waiting ever since.
Time you doubled-crossed me
You two-faced timer
I may not get you now
But I will get you yet
So help me God.
I didn't mind the wait
I didn't mind the climb
Success boy number one
I wanted the top so bad
I could taste it.
Everything I was, was in the future
Everything I owned, I sold for paradise
   Bye and bye.
My drive was blind.
All I ever wanted
Was everyone to say
He made it!
Double talking clock
You fibbing liar
Because of you

My home, my all
Was built on sand
The sands of time
That ran away
And left me hanging in the air
Without a past
Without a future
Out of touch with everyone
So long used to using others.
I wouldn't do it all again
For anyone else
EXCEPT myself!

(Mark 14:1)
"While they were at table eating, Jesus said, 'I tell you solemnly, one of you is about to betray me, one of you eating with me.'"

MONDAY OF HOLY WEEK

Lately I have come to think of God
   as a joker
Why else would he give us life and
   leave us?
Why else would he make the world
   and ask us to run it?
God is a chancer, with a fantastic
   love of humans
He delights to be with us,
His Son is one of us.
When we love and grow,
How He must laugh and smile,
When we hate and hurt
How He must cry!
Yes, he is a funny guy,
Our God, Our Father.
I love His sense of humor!
This three ring circus!
Life!

TUESDAY OF HOLY WEEK

My hands are too small to carry
 all I need.
My eyes are too weak to see all I know
 to be real
O God, I take seriously your signals
 from afar that I feel deep from within.
Something great is happening in life
And you invited me to take part in it.
I am the spit of God
His breath I breathe!
I believe in all that life is doing to me,
In all that has happened to me
I trust in where life leads me.
In deep and lonely moments I journey
 inward to my heart to the center of myself
And know that He is there where my
Love lives and my soul is.
I have found His presence, His Kingdom,
Within.

Saints of Heaven, help me a dreamer
 of heavenly dreams.
A human who follows after the humans
 who have gone before leaving me behind
 dreaming.
Move over friends, I will soon be coming
 over.
Watch out for me now from here to there
It is going to get tougher in the road ahead.

My God I believe,
Help Thou my unbelief.

This is the last hope,
Held out for a scattered people,
That someday, somehow
Things broken will be fixed
Friends parted will be gathered!
People long since dead shall hear again their song playing, and they will come back from their holes in the ground to sing it.

Faces will appear out of everywhere.
Faces we haven't seen for so long
We have forgotten that we ever knew.
At first they will seem greatly changed
But then that look, the voice, that smile, the wink
"And I'll be damned
If it isn't what's his name!"
This is the holy in our story book
That can be trusted
Herein lies the meaning of our broken lives
Our love is real
LIFE CAN BE TRUSTED!

WEDNESDAY OF HOLY WEEK

Once upon this world, on the very same night
Two men died.
One man's name was Judas,
The other man's name was Christ.
Judas died for the love of things,
And Jesus died for the love of people.

Christ, a man after God's own heart
Lived all His life for others.
And still, though very young,
He died fulfilled.

Judas lived for silver
 and feeling empty in the end,
Did himself in!
He was buried in a pauper's grave
The spot was left unmarked,
His grave is lost in grass.

Christ, his friend, left us with
 an empty tomb where billions since have
 come and gone to pray for that mighty
 grace *of always loving people.*
And always using things!

THURSDAY OF HOLY WEEK

It was the night before He was killed
That He said of bread
This is my body, which is given to you!
Of wine He said
This is my blood which is shed for you
   Do this in memory of me!
We have done it ever since with much love.
It was the last supper!
It was the first Mass!

There is more to Mass than bread and wine
There is more to man than flesh and blood
There is more to life than meets the eye
Something big is going on in the Universe
We live in the shadow of some great
   substance
We dwell in the shade of some eternal light
We are all in the real presence
Of a real presence.

Walk soft, tread gently—Oh men coming in
The ground on which you stand is holy
Here is Eucharist
This is the house of mysteries, built by men.
Things happen here that are never seen,
Words are said that are never heard
A million saints of nameless faces,
Kneel each day before this Mighty Bread
Where human knees wear out the floors of
   God.

Faces buried in their hands,
Their ears listening to the ground of being.
All lost—all found,
In the sights and sounds of another world.
Muttering words not meant for human
 listening
Each one stutters out to God
Their detailed situation.
Then quietly listen for that soft
 reply that is never said.
Finishing thus their unavailing prayers,
They bless themselves,
Genuflect and walk away.
Convinced that in the end everything will be
 okay.

A strange feeling this to be an outside witness
To man's closed sessions with his hidden
 savior.
A strange thing of terrible beauty
Is the whole world of religious carry-on
But it was ever thus, and shall be forever so.
A mannish thing to do to kneel and say one's
 prayers.
There is no house outside the world.
The world is in this house
No one will ever tell, for no one will ever
 know
What really happens here,
Between what looks like bread
And the clotted clots of human
 consciousness.
Inside these human heads,
Thousands come and thousands go,

Spilling into the chalice
The madness of their own peculiar world.

Like children simple and unashamed
They tell the tabernacle
Thoughts they dare not tell to another.
Here is where people place their trust
Against the constant fear of nothingness.
Here they find shelter from the
   swirling shambles of their world.
Here there is something to hold on to
When all they love is dying of time.
Here the silent wish is made
That life is up to something great.
Here is where those who have gone beyond
Meet with those they left behind.
Here their past and present stay,
Here their future is guaranteed.
At this cross roads of eternity and time
Through a glass darkly, they see Him.
Him in whom they live, move, and have
   their being, their Eucharist

GOOD FRIDAY

The park was named Gethsemane
A human figure shivered there
Lonely in the dark
His sweat turned red
Ran down upon his cloak
Was it nerves?
Or was it fright?
Not for nothing do men sweat blood
The night was quiet
Except for the snoring of his friends
And the hammering of some men
Setting up a cross
Upon a distant hill
His zero hour had come
The count-down had begun
He had to do the lonesome thing
He had to die
Like any other human
His heart recoiled
The usual concern occupied his mind
The question why?
Father let this pass,
He prayed
Not my will but thine be done
His prayers were heard
But nothing happened!
The soldiers came and carried him away.
And late next day upon the cross
At three o'clock he passed away.

The whispering people whispered 'round
Indeed, He was the Son of God
Frightened by the dread of what was done
They all ran home their separate ways
That night they woke in awful dreams
Crying in their sleep
Kneeling at their beds
They prayed to God that Jesus wouldn't
Haunt them.
But He did, not only them
But also us,
The rest is history!

PART II

In His moment of final violence, Christ's thoughts turned naturally to the people who peopled His world. His mother He gave to John, the thief at His side He promised heaven, for all His assassins He asked forgiveness, His awareness of others was with Him even on his death bed. His touch with Himself and the Father was just as real. "I thirst" He said and then in awful sorrow cried "My God, My God, why hast thou forsaken me" but then at the end "Into thy hand I give up my spirit." "It is finished." And so died a life of a love lived.

The Word of God made man
Is not hard to understand
It is only hard to take
And make his kind of love
A way of life!

HOLY SATURDAY

At this time in human events
The world is going through
"Her change of life."
In this period of vast
 dislocation
Words are violent!
Some call it treason
Some call it freedom
Some say it's calvary
Some say it's Easter
No one says it's easy.
Damned if you do
Damned if you don't
Insecurity is a fact of life
And everyone is caught
In the cross fire of rage
In the middle of free-
 floating hate.
Something has died
No one knows what!
Something is born
With difficult birth!
The faithful have
 scattered
To cover their hurt
Each to his own
 fall-out shelter
Everyone is to blame
Except the one who is to
 blame

God:
He is the one who has brought us out
Into this desert to die!
Or to trust!

Despite the creeds we mouth
Despite the prayers we say
   out loud
We are wary of what He
   is doing to us
By all He has let happen to us
And gingerly we follow
   where He leads us
Covering our tracks
In case we want to come back.

Like a teenager the whole
   human race
Is being dragged
   screaming
To our adult place
In a world come of age.
Tell the fishers of men
The good times have
   come
Their God is too small
The ballgame has changed
Another brand of saint
Is sought
With soul that is
   world size
This cut of man is
   not too large to live
He is happy washing feet

A loving servant
Who serves God's underworld
All he knows is that
   he doesn't know
All that is meant by
   what is said
He will never claim to understand
What men mean by what men do!
Yet indeed, it is a different
   kind of day
When we wake up to find
Our times are up to
   something great
Around the world
Again shall rise
The loud laugh of hope
That comes from faith
   in something
Greater than ourselves.
We shall live again
Like children playing
Accepting total joy
As our destined lot
We shall feel again love
   come alive in everyone.

The world will be the same
Yet living here will be
   different.
We will celebrate in
   wild fiesta
The promises already
   made

The promises already
   kept.
Our blood will boil again
   with gusto for a world saved.
We will dance together
   in the streets
And sing together
   in our parks.
When once again the impossible
   is real
Then again shall awe and
   wonder reign
Fascination and surprise
Excitement will invade
The churches
Jumping up and down
   in the pews
Waltzing in the aisles.
Cynics will melt to
   smiles
'Til tears run down
   their cheeks
We will be saved from
   ourselves
When we realize we are
   already saved
All we have got to do
Is celebrate!
And so:
And so:
The world waits,
Some for Godot!
Some for the Second Coming!

Oh! reader of words
Whoever you are
A word to remember
Is Easter!

Happy Hol-i-Days